MARGARITAS SANGRIAS & MORE!

Fiesta Drink Recipes for:
Margaritas, Frozen and On the Rocks,
Zesty Sangrias, Mellow Tequila Sunrises,
and much more!

GOLDEN
WEST ☼
PUBLISHERS

ISBN 13: 978-1-58581-021-5
ISBN 10: 1-58581-021-5

Printed in the United States of America

Illustrations: Sean Hoy
Cover and Interior Design: The Printed Page

Golden West Publishers
4113 N. Longview
Phoenix, AZ 85014
(800) 658-5830
(602) 265-4392

For free sample recipes from every Golden West cookbook visit:
www.goldenwestpublishers.com

CONTENTS

How Margaritaville was Founded!

The history of the "margarita" thrives on intrigue and conflict. Many contenders vie for the title of the creator of the Margarita Cocktail throughout the 1930s and 1940s.

One famous account sets the serving of the first Margarita in Old Town San Diego by Danny Negrete around 1936. The family story reveals that Danny opened a bar at the Garci Crispo Hotel with his brother, David. Danny presented the Margarita to David as a wedding gift the day before David's wedding! On that day the combination of the concoction was not blended and was served with hand-crushed ice.

Or you might like the story that in the 1940s a bartender in Texas, Pancho Morales in Tommy's Place, a Mex-Tex Juarez bar invented the famous tequila cocktail and called it a daisy or margarita. Another version of this invention is of the same bartender only in this tale, Pancho entered a national drink contest and he came up with the Margarita, which he named after his wife. He always served it on the rocks and it was not machine blended. Dipping the rim of the glass in salt was a mistake as Pancho meant to use sugar!

Another tale reveals Danny Herrera mixing a jigger of white tequila with lemon juice and Triple Sec in a bar, Rancho La Gloria, on an old road that connects Tijuana with Rosarito Beach. Danny added shaved ice and blended the mixture in a hand shaker creating a smooth concoction with salt!

Or you may choose the story of socialite, Margarita Sames, who came up with the Margarita cocktail at one of her famous Christmas parties at her vacation home in Acapulco. Among her guests at the party was Tommy Hilton, who then introduced the luscious Margarita cocktail to his hotel chain.

SEVEN MYTHS ABOUT TEQUILA

#1. Tequila is made from fermented cactus juice.

Tequila is made from the sugar-rich heart of the blue agave plant. The agave is a succulent related to the lily and amaryllis. It takes 8-10 years to mature, with a lifespan of up to 15 years. A mature agave can reach 7-12 feet in diameter, with leaves from 5 to 8 feet tall. The agave hearts, called piñas, are usually harvested when they are 50-80 pounds, however, they can weigh as much as 300 pounds and more. The sap from the roasted piñas is fermented and double, or triple distilled in the tequila producing process.

#2. Tequila has medicinal properties.

Tequila is considered healthy when used in moderation; however, there are no firm research results, or scientific evidence to confirm the medicinal properties of either tequila or the agave plant.

#3. All tequilas are the same.

Tequilas vary much like wines due to the growing environment and the process used for production. Many factors affect the flavor and body of the tequila including soil, region, temperature and the age of the agave at harvesting. Another factor relates to the equipment used and the process by which the distiller bakes and ages its final product.

Tequila's wide variation of flavors extends across brands and between the styles: blanco, reposado and añejo. It is sometimes very difficult for beginning aficionados to recognize and appreciate the varied distinctions. Traditional production methods generally produce much stronger agave flavor than modern, mass production. Barrel aging has a significant impact on the color and taste as tequila, again like wine, picks up the very essence of the wood from the barrel.

#4. Tequila and Mezcal are the same thing.

Tequila is a "type" of mezcal, however, mezcals are not tequilas. Tequila is made only from the *blue* agave that is produced in a specific region of Mexico. Its name came from the little town of "Tequila" in the state of Jalisco, Mexico. Mezcal can be made from five varieties of agave.

#5. Tequila is only bottled homebrew.

Carefully distilled and aged, tequila is not "moonshine." The Mexican government and the Tequila Regulatory Council tightly control the manufacturing of tequila. Information stated on a bottle of tequila regarding its age, content and style have rigid legal requirements. In addition, the Chamber of Tequila Producers, a not-for-profit council, tightly regulates the tequila industry.

Most tequila producers take great pride in their production and some limited añejo varieties are aged for approximately four years in oak barrels.

All of this is not to say that there aren't local home brews distilled from the agave sap and a lot of these are considered regional drinks, legal for production only in Mexico.

#6. There is a worm in tequila.

There is no worm in tequila that is bottled in Mexico. If you find a bottle of tequila with a worm it is probably not worth drinking!

How the worm wiggled its way into the tequila story …

 It's a known fact…tourists are often too trusting. Especially when traveling without ample knowledge of language or customs. Stopping for a local libation, we tend to allow our friendly natives to guide and beguile us…which is how the worm wiggled its way into the tequila realm.

First, you need to know that according to tequila purists, genuine tequila *never* includes a worm—despite the affable barkeep's claim. Only mezcal may contain the squiggly creature, which is an agave worm, a.k.a., butterfly larvae. The little guy goes where the sweets are, into the heart of the agave plant and mezcal bottlers insist it adds flavor to the liquor. Yum.

But, it isn't like you can order a can of worms for lunch at the local deli…how did eating the worm at the bottom of the bottle become a delicacy, and in some rowdy situations a rite of passage? And how did the coral (considered tastiest) or plump white worm find himself swimming in a bottle, anyway? Marketing makes the world go 'round, or in this case, the worm go down. Embellishing only slightly, it is said that in the 1950s young Jacobo Lozano Paez, a Mexico City entrepreneur, was bottling mezcal when along came a couple of adventurous tourists seeking some native flavor. Eager to please, Paez dropped a worm into the bottle and banked on the Aztec legend that the *gusan rojo* worms were an aphrodisiac and, well…the worm didn't stand a chance.

Generally considered a pest at that time, the winsome worm's reputation grew and these days they are actually raised and sent around the world, to be the crowning glory to a fine bottle of mezcal. Bottom's up!

LinDee Rochelle

#7. The best tequilas cost the most.

A high-priced bottle of tequila doesn't always mean it's the best! Tequila has become a "collector's item," thus a portion of the price of a bottle of tequila may be in its fancy packaging and designer bottling. Let your tequila taste buds lead you, not your wallet, when choosing your next bottle of tequila!

THE FOUR TYPES OF TEQUILA

TYPE ONE:

Blanco or plata is white or silver and is the most common type. It's under 60 days old, is not aged, and is sometimes bottled right from distillation. Even if it is not aged, this tequila is 100% agave and can be tastier and more robust than highly refined varieties. Blanco may be "rested" in oak barrels in some distilleries for a maximum period allowed of 30 days.

TYPE TWO:

Joven abocado is young and smoothed, and is also called gold tequila. This variety is basically the same as with blanco, added ingredients for coloring and flavoring, making it look aged. They're known as mixto, or mixed blends, in the industry and may have been distilled from as little as 60% agave juice with other sugars. As a general rule, they don't measure up to the 100% agave tequilas.

TYPE THREE:

Reposado means rested in Spanish. Reposado "rests" or is aged from two months to up to a year in oak casks or barrels. This is where the better tequilas start and the tastes become richer and more complex. The coloring becomes darker with age, as well as becoming more intensely affected by the wood. Reposado was the first type of aged tequila.

TYPE FOUR:

Añejo means aged, or vintage and is matured in government-sealed barrels with no more than 350 liters, for a minimum of one year. Many experts say tequila is at its best when aged for four or five years. Many of the añejos become quite dark and the influence of the wood is more pronounced than in the reposado variety.

Reserva de casa, an unofficial "type," usually refers to premium tequila. They are mostly añejo and may be presented as limited production varieties. Reserva de casa should be identified as 100% agave.

All tequilas have a similar alcohol content, which is roughly the same percentage as any standard scotch, vodka, gin or bourbon at around 38%-40%, or 76 to 80 proof.

IDENTIFYING YOUR TEQUILA OF CHOICE

In making a decision about your choice of tequila, it may require testing several brands and a variety of types to find the taste that suits you. Some distilleries have reputations for making mild, spicy or earthy brands, while others have a strong alcohol finish, and still others represent a range of various tastes.

Go for a "tequila tasting"! Find yourself a good bartender who knows his stuff in the varieties of tequila. You'll find marked differences between the reposados of Hussong's, which have a very strong agave flavor; the El Tesoro, which has a solid body and very mellow aroma; the Hornitos lends a peppery bite and a long finish; and, the Herradura, which is very mellow and has a distinct smoothness.

In looking at tequila labels, the most important identifier on the label is "100% agave" or "100% agave azul"—cien por ciento de agave azul. This tells you that the tequila is made only from the blue agave plant and has been approved by a government inspector ensuring its purity. If this information is not on the label, the tequila in the bottle legally can be mixed with up to 49% of "other" ingredients, often referred to as a "mixto."

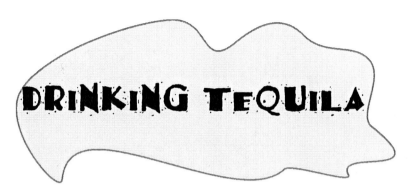

DRINKING TEQUILA

The traditional way to drink tequila is in a tall, narrow shot glass called a caballito or tequilito—little horse or pony. The caballito has a narrow base with a bit wider mouth and is said to be designed after the original bull's horn from which tequila was consumed. The bottom was cut flat so it could rest on a table. It's a perfect size and shape.

Most people think of tequila as a "shooter," however, you can certainly embrace it and sip it as you would a fine liqueur. Forget the lime and salt and throw out the margarita mix just once!

Try it chilled… especially the blanco variety. However, if it's appreciation for the full bouquet and body of tequila you desire, then sip it at room temperature.

MARGARITA TRIVIA

❖ The world's first margarita machine was invented in 1971 by a restaurateur from Dallas. It can be seen today at the Smithsonian Natural Museum of American History.

❖ The preferred salt for Margaritas is kosher salt, which has a cleaner and milder taste than table salt.

❖ Some sources state the word *margarita* means "daisy" in Spanish and "pearl" in Latin.

❖ A Margarita can contain up to 500 calories! That is almost four times more than a martini (120 calories) and substantially more than a piña colada (312 calories).

MARGARITAS

- ❖ Variations of Margaritas
- ❖ How to Make the Perfect Margarita
- ❖ To Salt or Not to Salt…

VARIATIONS OF MARGARITAS

Straight Up: Combine ingredients with ice in a shaker. Shake 20-30 times then strain into a chilled martini or margarita glass. Garnish with a fresh lime slice.

On the Rocks: Combine ingredients with ice in a shaker, shake until mixed, then strain into martini or margarita glass filled with ice. Garnish with a lemon wheel.

Frozen: Unless otherwise instructed, combine ingredients in blender with 1 cup of ice. Blend until smooth. Pour into glass and serve with a fresh wedge of lime.

Frozen Fruit Margaritas: Blenders are magical when it comes to margaritas! You can literally purée any fresh fruit that your little heart desires and make your margarita simply lip smackin' good! If you want to further enhance your frozen fruit margarita, add a liqueur that "matches" the fresh fruit…for example, if you're using raspberries use a raspberry liqueur… get the picture? Fresh peaches with peach Schnapps. Have fun, as these are delightfully refreshing drinks!

HOW TO MAKE A PERFECT MARGARITA

- ❖ First moisten the rim of the glass with lime
- ❖ Salt the rim of the glass
- ❖ Fill the glass with ice to chill
- ❖ Combine the tequila, orange liqueur and lime juice in an ice-filled shaker
- ❖ Shake it up, Baby!
- ❖ Pour the contents into the chilled margarita glass
- ❖ Garnish with a slice of lime
- ❖ Salud!

TO SALT OR NOT TO SALT... THAT IS THE QUESTION!

Many people find that a salt rim enhances the flavor of the margarita.

To salt glasses, rub the rim of the glass with lime or lemon then gently dip into saucer laced with kosher or fine sea salt. Remember to salt the rim before it is filled with ice or ingredients.

But wait... what about sugar? Or a combination of sugar and salt? Hey, it's your margarita! Guess what... you can do whatever fits your taste buds, so try some combinations and see what mixes up as your favorite. You'll find that salt fits some recipes and sugar fits with others and a combo is just dandy in some particular instances. Enjoy and Salud!

CLASSIC MARGARITA

1 ½ cups **Tequila**
1 ½ cups **Lime Juice**
1 cup **Triple Sec**
2 cups crushed **Ice**
6 **Lime Slices**

Combine tequila, juice, triple sec and ice in shaker. Shake well. Pour into 6 salt-rimmed glasses and add lime to each. Serves 6.

The margarita is a classic favorite of the Southwest. They are traditionally served in salt-rimmed cocktail glasses. To prepare the glasses, rub the rims with lemon or lime juice and dip into salt. Chill until serving time.

FRUIT FLAVORED MARGARITA

Margarita recipe (see previous page)
Fresh Fruit, if available or **Fruit Flavored Liqueur**

Prepare Classic Margarita according to directions. Add fresh fruit of choice or liqueur to margarita. Blend together.

SUZYQ'S SUMMER MARGARITA

Susan Sheehan, Bay Shore, New York

2 oz. **Agave Tequila**   4 oz. **Seltzer**
1 tsp. **Limeade Concentrate**   **Tangerine Wedge**

Combine tequila, limeade concentrate and seltzer. Shake well. Pour over ice and squeeze with tangerine wedge. Serves 1.

BLUE SKIES MARGARITA

5 oz. **Tequila**
3 oz. **Blue Curacao**
2 oz. **Rum**
2 cups **Sour Mix**
Optional: **Sliced limes** and **lemons** for garnish

Make sure that all ingredients are well chilled before mixing! Mix all of the ingredients together in a small pitcher. Serve immediately in chilled glasses. Serves 2-3.

IT'S A PURPLE CATALINA MARGARITA

The combination of the blue Curacao and the Peach Schnapps turns this concoction "purple"! Be careful, this purple people eater will sneak up on you!

1 1/2 oz. **Tequila**
1/2 oz. **Blue Curacao**
1 oz. **Peach Schnapps**
4 oz. **Sour Mix**
Orange Slices for garnish

Shake with ice. Serve in sugar-rimmed margarita glasses garnished with an orange slice. Serves 1.

Note: You can make this a blended drink if you'd like… it slides down even easier when blended!

CHRISTMAS MARGARITA

1 1/2 oz. **Tequila**
1 oz. **Rose's Lime Juice**®
1 1/2 oz. **Triple Sec**
1 1/2 oz. **Sweet and Sour Mix**
2 oz. **Cranberry Juice**
Orange Slices and fresh **Cranberries** for garnish

Optional: **Red Sugar**

Combine all ingredients with ice in blender and mix until smooth. Serve in a margarita glass garnished with an orange slice. Pop a couple of fresh cranberries on top when serving, to add color. As an option for sparkling festivity, dip the rim in red colored sugar! Serves 1.

WATERMELON MARGARITA

16 oz. **Watermelon**, seeded and blended
1/2 fresh **Lime**
6 oz. **Tequila**
3 oz. **Triple Sec**
1 Tablespoon **Sugar**

Cut up watermelon, removing seeds. Mix in blender until you have about 16 ounces of watermelon liquid. If watermelon is not sweet enough, add sugar to taste. Add all remaining ingredients. Top blender with ice, continue blending until smooth. Pour into chilled glasses rimmed in sugar. Serves 2.

First Frozen Margarita Machine Mix
The first frozen Margarita machine mix was invented in 1971 for the Dallas restaurant, Marianos, by chemist John Hogan. He was also recognized by the Smithsonian Institute as the inventor of the frozen Margarita machine.

FROSTY LEMON MARGARITA

1 cup **Lime-Flavored Mineral Water**
1/4 to 1/2 cup **Tequila**, to taste
1 pint **Lemon Sorbet**
Mint Leaves for garnish

Combine all ingredients in blender and mix at high speed just until smooth. Serve immediately in chilled glasses. Garnish with a mint leaf, if desired. Serves 3-4.

COCONUT MARGARITA

1 cup **Ice**
2 oz. **Tequila**
1/4 cup **Coco Lopez**
3 tbsp. fresh **Lime Juice**

Place all ingredients in a blender and mix until smooth.
Serves 1.

ORANGE MARGARITA

1 oz. **Tequila**
1/2 oz. **Triple Sec**
6 oz. **Orange Juice**
Splash of **Lime Juice**

Combine all ingredients, except lime juice, over ice and stir. Serve with a splash of lime juice and forget the salt on this one! Serves 1.

SiNG-ALONG-WiTH-TEQUILA

Songs about tequila and margaritas:

- *Tequila* — Youngbloodz
- *Tequila Sunrise* — Eagles
- *The Tequila Man* — Chuck Rio
- *Straight Tequila Night* — John Anderson
- *Tequila Town* — Brooks & Dunn
- *Pour Me Another Tequila* — Eddie Rabbitt
- *Tequila Talkin'* — Lonestar
- *Margaritaville* — Jimmy Buffett

MANGO MARGARITA
(Blended)

1 oz. **Mango Puree**
1 1/2 oz. **Tequila**
2 oz. **Margarita Mix**
1 oz. **Lime Juice**
1/2 oz. **Countreau**

Mix ingredients in a blender for 30 seconds. Pour into a chilled glass topped with salt. Serves 1.

PRICKLY PEAR MARGARITA

1 1/2 oz. **Patron Añejo Tequila**
2 oz. **Margarita Mix**
1 oz. **Lime Mix**
1 oz. **Prickly Pear Mix**
1 oz. **Triple Sec**

Place ice in shaker. Add ingredients and shake thoroughly for approximately 15 seconds. Rim glass with salt. Pour ingredients into glass and serve with lime as a garnish. Serves 1.

CADILLAC MARGARITA

1 1/2 oz. **Don Julio® Tequila**
1 oz. **Orange Juice**
2 oz. **Margarita Mix**
1 oz. **Lime Juice**
1 oz. **Triple Sec**
Grand Marnier to taste

Mix ingredients in shaker; pour contents into chilled margarita glass with salted rim and float with Grand Marnier. Serves 1.

WATERMELON MARGARITA II

Sondra Grandy, Cottonwood, Arizona

- 4 cups **Seedless Watermelon**, cubed
- 2 cups **Ice**
- 2 tbsp. **Sugar**
- 2 **Limes** (squeezed for juice)
- 1/2 cup **Tequila**
- 2 Tbsp. **Triple Sec**

Place watermelon, ice, sugar and lime juice into the blender. Mix on slow speed. Next, add tequila and triple sec; blend again.

Wet rims of glasses, dip in sea salt and pour blended mixture into glasses. Serves 4-6.

MARGARITA POMEGRANATE-STYLE!

2 oz. **Pomegranate Juice**
1 oz. **Lime Juice**
3 oz. **Tequila**
2 oz. **Triple Sec**
1 tbsp. **Grenadine**
1/2 fresh **Orange**

Use two margarita glasses and wet the rims with a little juice from the orange. Roll the outside edges of the rim in salt. Place all the ingredients in a cocktail shaker with ice cubes and gently shake until mixture is cold. Slice half the orange and place each slice on the edge of the glass. Drop a few pomegranate seeds into each glass and enjoy! Serves 2.

Beer-Garita

1 can **Fresca**
1 can **Mexican Beer**
1 large can **Frozen Limeade**
1/2 limeade can **Water**
3/4 limeade can **Tequila**

Mix together and serve on the rocks. Serves 6.

SANGRIAS

SANGRIA'S HISTORIC TALE

The origins of the sangria, a traditional red wine punch, can be traced to Spain and Portugal in the 1700s, where it was first developed. It then spread across Europe becoming increasingly popular.

The word sangria comes from the Spanish root word, "sangre" meaning blood. However, some sangrias are made with white wine, better known as "Sangria Blanco."

During the sangria's early years, the Claret, a Bordeaux from France, was the dominant ingredient and base for most recipes. Others utilized a Rioja, a red wine from

Spain. Next, they added brandy and fruit for flavoring. It was quite a hit at parties during this era!

If visiting the southern region of Spain, you may be served a sangria called "Zurra," which is made with peaches and nectarines. Nowadays, many restaurants have created their own sangria recipes. It continues to generally consist of the following standard ingredients: a red wine, sliced or chopped fruit, honey or orange juice as a sweetener and usually brandy, triple sec, or other liquor.

TIPS WHEN SERVING SANGRIA

Sangria has wine and fruit thus can decay rapidly when warm. Wine also turns to vinegar quite quickly once exposed to the air, and fruit can get mushy and begin to fall apart. Therefore, it is best to keep sangria refrigerated. When serving it in the pitcher, use ice cubes. Plastic ice cubes are effective and will not melt to dilute your drink.

It is recommended to drink sangria within a day or two to prevent a vinegar flavor from permeating the punch. Drink up and enjoy!

CLASSIC SANGRIA

Sangria is a sweet punch or cooler that, like the margarita, has endless varieties and flavors.

1 bottle **Rosé Wine**
½ cup **Tequila**
1 cup **Orange Juice**
¼ cup **Sugar**
2 **Limes,** sliced very thin

Combine wine, tequila, orange juice and sugar. Mix well. Pour over ice cubes. Add lime slices to each glass. Dilute with orange or lemon-lime soda, if desired. Serves 6.

SPARKLING SANGRIA

Sangria is favorite drink throughout the Southwest.

2 bottles (750 ml) **Dry Red** or **Rosé Wine**
1 cup **Sugar**
2 **Oranges**, sliced very thin
1 **Lemon**, sliced very thin
1 **Lime**, sliced very thin
2 bottles (10 oz. each) **Club Soda**

Combine all ingredients and chill well. Serve in tall glasses over ice. Makes 2 quarts.

SANGRIA PUNCH

1 bottle (fifth) **Burgundy Wine**
2 cups fresh **Orange Juice**
1 **Orange**, sliced
1 **Lemon**, sliced
1 **Lime**, sliced
2 to 4 cups chilled **Ginger Ale**

Combine wine, orange juice and fruit slices in large pitcher. Chill. Before serving, add ginger ale, as desired. Serves 8 or more.

SOUTH OF THE BORDER SANGRIA

8 oz. **Pinot Grigio**
4 oz. **Merlot**
4 oz. **Triple Sec**
4 oz. **Orange Juice**
2 **Oranges**, segmented
1 **Lemon**, sliced
1 **Lime**, sliced

Combine all ingredients except fruit. Chill overnight. Add fruit before serving. Pour over ice and serve. Perfect for summertime temperatures! Serves 4.

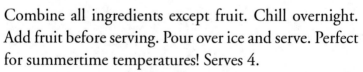

LOST NIGHT "SANGRITA"

2 cups freshly-squeezed **Orange Juice**
3 tbsp. **Grenadine**
1/4 tsp. **Chili Powder,** to taste
1 cup **Tomato Juice** (optional)
3 tsp. **Salt***

1 1/2 oz. **Tequila**

Combine all ingredients together except the tequila. Mix well. Next, pour tequila into a large glass over ice cubes. Add the "Sangrita" mixture to the glass of tequila. If desired, add club soda. Garnish with a lime wedge. Serves 2-4.

* If you omit the tomato juice, use 2 teaspoons of salt.

LOLITA SANGRIA

1/2 cup **Dry White Wine**
1/4 cup **Club Soda**
1/2 oz. **Triple Sec**
1 **Orange Slice**
1 **Red Grape**
1 **Watermelon Wedge**
1 **Cherry**

Mix together and serve over ice. Serves 1.

SANGRIA FOR A CROWD

Debbie Kauzlarich, Chicago, Illinois

3 bottles inexpensive **Spanish Red Wine**
1 cup **Brandy**
1/4-1/2 cup **Cointreau** or **Triple Sec**
1 quart **Orange Juice** (no pulp is best)
1 cup **Lemon Juice**
1/2-1 cup superfine **Sugar**
Red or **White Grapes** (or both)
1 **Orange**, thinly sliced
2 **Lemons**, thinly sliced
2 **Limes**, thinly sliced
1 can **Chunky Pineapple**, drained
1 **Apple**, diced
1-2 bottles **Lemon-Lime Soda**

continued on the next page

Pour the wine, brandy and Cointreau into a large punch bowl. Stir orange and lemon juice with the sugar until sugar has dissolved. Then add to bowl and stir to blend. Add fruit and chill overnight.

When serving, make sure to have some of the fruit in each glass. Put in a few ice cubes, top with sangria, leaving a few inches at the top. Pour in the soda, give a quick stir and enjoy.

Don't mix the soda in the big bowl of sangria because you will have a ton of sangria and if you don't drink it all, the soda goes flat. It's better to add it at the end.

Note: You don't have to use a really good brandy! You can use any or all of the fruit to taste—or add only the fruit that you like.

ISLAND SANGRIA

Sugar to taste
2 cups **Apple Juice**
2 tbsp. **Lemon Juice**
1 bottle dry **White Wine**
1 cup **Pineapple Cubes**
1 sour **Apple**
1 bottle **Ginger Ale**
12 **Ice Cubes**

In a pitcher, dissolve the sugar in the apple juice. Add lemon juice, wine, pineapple and apple in chunks. Mix. Add ginger ale and ice right before serving. Serves 8-12.

FIESTA SANGRIA

2 gallons **Red Wine** of choice (Burgundy, Merlot, Shiraz, Cabernet Sauvignon)
1 pint **Brandy**
1 pint **Rum**
3 quarts **Club Soda** or **Lemon-Lime Soda**
1 **Orange**, slice thin

Combine wine, brandy, rum and soda of choice. Mix well. Add sliced oranges to float on top. Chill. Serves 8-16.

HOT AND SAUCY SANGRIA

  1 bottle (750 ml) **Red Wine** of choice
  2 tsp. **Lemon Juice**
  2 tsp. **Lime Juice**
  4 tsp. **Orange Juice**
  2 tbsp. **Sugar**
  2 tsp. **Hot Sauce** of choice
  1 shot **Rum**
  1 bottle (16 oz.) **Club Soda**

Pour all ingredients into serving pitcher. Mix well. Chill until ready to serve. Serves 8.

PACKS A PUNCH SANGRIA

- 1 liter **Sweet Red Wine**
- 3/4 liter **Sherry**
- 1/4 liter **Watermelon Schnapps**
- 1/4 liter **Blackcurrant Schnapps**
- 1/4 liter **Grapefruit Schnapps**
- 1/4 liter **Brandy**
- 1 liter **Fruit juice** (preferably a Sangria fruit juice mix)
- 1/2 liter **Lemon-Lime Soda**
- 1 bag **Ice**

Mixing instructions: Mix all the ingredients together in a large pitcher. Once thoroughly blended, add the ice and serve in wine glasses. Serves 8-16.

SLAP HAPPY PEACH SANGRIA

1 small **Lemon,** sliced thin
1 small **Orange,** sliced thin
3 tbsp. **Granulated Sugar**
1 **Peach,** peeled, sliced thin
1/4 cup **Peach Schnapps**
1 bottle (750 ml) **White Wine,** chilled
Strawberries and **Kiwi Fruit** for garnish

Combine all the ingredients in a pitcher. Stir the sangria until the sugar is dissolved. Chill for 1 hour. Strain the sangria into wine glasses and garnish with strawberries and sliced kiwi fruit. Serves 4.

GRAND MARNIER SANGRIA

1 bottle (750 mil) **Cabernet Sauvignon**
2/3 cup **Grand Marnier**
8 **Cherries,** sliced
2 **Oranges,** segmented
1 **Lemon,** cut into wedges
1 **Lime,** cut into wedges

Place all ingredients in serving pitcher. Chill overnight until ready to serve. Strain and serve over ice. Serves 4.

ORANGE SANGRIA

1 bottle (750 ml) **Red Wine** of choice (Burgundy,
  Merlot, Shiraz, Cabernet Sauvignon, Rioja,
  Zinfandel)
Juice of 1 **Lemon**, fresh squeezed
Juice of 1 **Orange**, fresh squeezed
Juice of 1 **Lime**, fresh squeezed
2 tbsp. **Sugar**
1 tbsp. **Orange Juice**
1/4 cup **Gin**
1 quart **Ginger Ale**
1 cup sliced **Strawberries**
1 cup diced **Pineapples**

Combine wine, fresh squeezed fruit juices and diced
pineapple. Mix thoroughly. Add sugar, orange juice and
gin. Chill overnight. Add ginger ale, berries and ice
before serving. Stir until well blended. Serves 6-8.

California Blueberry Sangria

1 bottle (750 ml) **California White Shiraz Wine**
1 **Lime,** cut into wedges
1 **Orange,** cut into wedges
2 tbsp. **Sugar**
2 shots **Brandy**
2 cups **Club Soda**
1 cup fresh or frozen **Blueberries**

Pour wine into serving pitcher. Squeeze juice from lime and orange wedges into wine. Reserve wedges. Add sugar, brandy and club soda. Mix well. Chill overnight. Add fruit wedges and blueberries before serving. Serves 6.

PEACH SANGRIA

1 bottle (750 ml) **Chablis** or **Chardonnay Wine**
2 shots **Rum**
1/2 cup **Sugar**
1 cup **Orange Juice**
Juice 1 **Lemon**, fresh squeezed
Juice 1 **Lime**, fresh squeezed
1 liter **Ginger Ale**
2 **Peaches**, sliced

Pour wine into serving pitcher. Add rum, sugar, orange juice, lemon and lime juice, and ginger ale. Mix well. Add peach slices. Chill until ready to serve. Serves 8-10.

KAHLÚA AND COFFEE DRINKS

Kahlúa is a liqueur that has the taste of both coffee and chocolate. It is made with coffee beans, cocoa beans and vanilla. With its bold flavor, only small amounts are needed in cocktails.

CAFÉ DE OLLA

Mexico is famous for its exceptional coffee.
Coffee is a widely used addition to many recipes.

4 cups strongly brewed **Coffee**
3 cups **Light Cream**
1/3 cup **Brandy**
1/3 cup **Rum**
1/3 cup **Creme de Cacao**

Simmer together in large pan, preferably earthenware.
Do not allow to boil. Serves 6.

KAHLÚA AFTER DINNER

1 pint **Vanilla Ice Cream**, softened
½ cup **Kahlúa® Coffee Liqueur**
1 cup black **Coffee**

Combine all ingredients in blender and mix well. Serve
in mugs. Serves 4.

STRAWBERRY KAHLÚA

Kahlúa is a drink that is delicious and versatile.
Choose fresh, ripe strawberries for best results.

3 cups fresh **Strawberries**, hulled
1 cup **Whipping Cream**
¼ cup **Kahlúa® Coffee Liqueur**

Combine all the ingredients in a blender. Mix thoroughly. Chill until ready to serve. Pour into sherbet cups. Serves 4.

HOMEMADE KAHLÚA

Wilma Travis, Crystal, Minnesota

2 cups **Water**
4 cups **Sugar**
1/4 cup **Instant Coffee**
1 pint **Vodka** or **Brandy**
1 **Vanilla Bean**

Boil sugar and water. Add coffee and cool. Next, add vodka or brandy. Pour into a 1/2 gallon bottle. Add vanilla bean. Place in tightly covered container and store in a cool, dry place for 2 months to age.

COFFEE LIQUEUR

4 cups **Sugar**
1/2 cup **Instant Coffee**
3 cups **Bottled Water** (preferable distilled)
1/4 tsp. **Salt**
2 1/2 cups **Vodka**, 80 proof
3 tbsp. **Vanilla Extract**

In large saucepan, stir sugar and coffee together. Add water and salt, place over high heat, stirring constantly until sugar is dissolved. Reduce heat, simmer for 1 hour. Remove from heat, stir in vodka and vanilla. Let cool. Store in tightly covered container. Makes 1 1/2 quarts.

Note: In addition to being served as a liqueur, this also makes a great topping for ice cream and fruit compote.

BUSHWACKER

Mari Beth Smith, University Heights, Ohio

4 oz. **Cream of Coconut**
2 oz. **Kahlúa® Coffee Liqueur**
1 oz. **Black Rum**
1 oz. **Creme de Cacao**
4 oz. **Half-and-Half**
Vanilla Ice Cream (optional)

Pour all ingredients into a blender (ice cream optional) with two cups of ice, and blend until mixed. Serve in a hurricane glass.

BANANA BLEND

20 ml. **Kahlúa**® **Coffee Liqueur**
20 ml. **Baileys**® **Irish Cream**
30 ml. **Cream**
One whole **Banana** (small size)

Use a banana that has been in the refrigerator for 24 hours. Blend all the ingredients together until very light and smooth. Serve in a tall cocktail glass and sit back and relax.

SMOOTH RUM & KAHLÚA®
COFFEE LIQUEUR

15 ml **Dark Rum**
15 ml **Kahlúa® Coffee Liqueur**
30 ml **Coconut Cream**
30 ml. **Fresh Cream**
1/2 **Banana**, refrigerated
Ice, crushed
Mint Leaves for garnish

Gently blend all of the ingredients until cold and smooth.
Pour into a tall glass and garnish with mint leaves.

KAHLÚA® BLACK RUSSIAN

2 parts **Kahlúa® Coffee Liqueur**
1 part **Stolichnaya® Vodka**

Pour over ice. Try it with Stolichnaya® Vanil or Stolichnaya® Razberi.

KAHLÚA® WHITE RUSSIAN

2 parts **Kahlúa® Coffee Liqueur**
1 part **Stolichnaya® Vodka**
Milk or **Cream**

Pour over ice. Try it with Stolichnaya® Vanil or Stolichnaya® Razberi.

Also try a Skinny White Russian with skim or soy milk.

KAHLÚA® MUDSLIDE

1 part **Kahlúa® Coffee Liqueur**
1 part **Stolichnaya® Vodka**
1/2 part **Irish Cream Liqueur**
1 part **Cream** or **Milk**

Combine all ingredients in a blender, mix well. Add ice and blend until smooth.

Try it with Stolichnaya® Vanil or Stolichnaya® Razberi, or Malibu Caribbean Rum®.

KAHLÚA® AND MILK

1 part **Kahlúa® Coffee Liqueur**
Milk or **Cream**

Mix together well. Pour over ice.
Serves 1.

KAHLÚA® RAZBERI WHITE RUSSIAN

2 parts **Kahlúa®** Coffee Liqueur
1 part **Stolichnaya®** Razberi Vodka
Milk or **Cream**
Raspberries for garnish

Mix all ingredients together. Pour over ice. Garnish with raspberries.

KAHLÚA® VANIL WHITE RUSSIAN

2 parts **Kahlúa®** Coffee Liqueur
1 part **Stolichnaya®** Vanil Vodka
Milk or **cream**
Vanilla Bean and **Mint Leaf** for garnish

Mix all ingredients together. Pour over ice. Garnish with vanilla beans and mint leaf.

KAHLÚA® EGGNOG

2 parts **Kahlúa® Coffee Liqueur**
1 part **Stolichnaya® Vodka**
Prepared Eggnog
Cinnamon Stick or **Mint Sprig** for garnish

Mix all ingredients together. Pour over ice. Garnish with cinnamon stick and/or mint sprig.

TEQUILA DRINKS

NACO SPECIAL

2 cups **Tomato** or **V-8**® **Vegetable Juice**
1 tbsp. **Lime Juice**
1 tsp. **Worcestershire Sauce**
1/2 cup **Tequila**

Combine all ingredients and shake well with ice.

The town of Tequila was founded in 1530 by Captain Cristobal de Onate, a Spanish Conquistador.

TEQUILA DAIQUIRI

½ cup **Tequila**
1 tsp. **Sugar**
¼ cup **Lime Juice**

Combine ingredients with ice and shake well. Pour into chilled glasses.

TEQUILA SUNRISE

1 1/3 cups **Orange Juice**
1/4 cup **Lime Juice**
1/2 cup **Tequila**
2 1/2 tsp. **Grenadine**
Mint Sprigs for garnish

Combine orange and lime juices with tequila. Pour into three ice-filled glasses. Slowly add grenadine to each glass. Add a sprig of fresh mint to each glass. Serves 3.

Tequila means "the rock that cuts." This phrase probably originated from the fact that the town is surrounded by obsidian (a sharp rock that was created by hot lava).

TUTTI FRUTTI

1 can (6 oz.) frozen **Orange Juice**
1 can (6 oz.) frozen **Limeade**
6 oz. **Tequila**, **Rum** or **Bourbon**
2 cups **Ice Cubes**
4 whole **Strawberries**

Combine ingredients, except strawberries, in blender and mix. Add ice cubes, a few at a time, until all are liquefied. Pour into old fashioned glasses and top with whole strawberry. Serves 4.

There are 136 species of agave in Mexico and about 30 different alcoholic beverages made from agave

TEQUILA CHRISTMAS COFFEE

1 bottle **Blanco Tequila**
1 package (6 oz.) **Raisins**
2 **Cinnamon Sticks**
16 oz. **Coffee**, brewed

In a pitcher, add tequila, raisins and cinnamon sticks. Mix well and chill in refrigerator for 3 hours.

Pour tequila mix into 16 oz. brewed coffee. Serve with sugar and cream. Serves 6-8.

STRAWBERRY TEQUILA

1 quart fresh **Strawberries**, halved
1 quart **Tequila**

Fill a quart jar with fresh strawberries. Pour tequila over strawberries until jar is filled. Cover tightly and store in dark closet for two weeks. Strain and serve as a liqueur.

Note: This delightful liqueur can be made with any fresh berries.

*The name **agave** comes from the Greek word for "noble."*

TEQUILA MARTINI COCKTAIL

1 1/2 oz. **Reposado** or **Añejo Tequila**
Splash of **Cointreau**

Add ingredients and shake with ice; strain into a chilled cocktail glass. Garnish with a twist of orange peel.

---

*Sauza's Hornitos derives its name from the **horno**, the traditional stone or brick oven used to soften piñas.*

TEQUILA SLUSH

1 ½ cups **Tequila**
1 can (6 oz.) frozen **Limeade**
1 cup **Orange Juice**
1 cup crushed **Ice** (or about 10-12 ice cubes)

Place in blender and mix on high until well blended and slushy. Serves 4.

TEQUILA CHRISTMAS CAKE

Try this one at your own risk!

1 cup **Water**	**Lemon Juice**
1 tsp. **Baking soda**	4 large **Eggs**
1 cup **Sugar**	**Nuts**
1 tsp. **Salt**	1 bottle **Tequila**
1 cup **Brown Sugar**	2 cups **Dried Fruit**

Sample the tequila to check quality.

Take a large bowl, check the tequila again to be sure it is of the highest quality, pour one level cup and drink.

Repeat.

Turn on the electric mixer.

Beat one cup of butter in a large fluffy bowl.

Add one teaspoon of sugar. Beat again.

At this point it's best a make sure the tequila is still OK. Try another cup…just in case.

Turn off the mixerer thingy.

Break 2 leggs and add to the bowl and chuck in the cup of dried fruit.

Pick the fruit up off the floor.

Mix on the turner.

If the fried druit gets stuck in the beaterers just pry it loose with a drewscriver.

Sample the tequila to check for tonsisticity.

Next, sift two cups of salt. Or something.

Check the tequila.

Now shift the lemon juice and strain the nuts.

Add one table.

Add a spoon of sugar, or some fink. Whatever you can find.

Greash the oven.

Turn the cake tin 360 degrees and try not to fall over.

Finally, throw the bowl through the window.

Finish the tequila and wipe counter with the cat.

TEQUILA SHOOTERS

BULL BY THE HORNS

1/2 oz. **Blanco Tequila**   1/2 oz. **Vodka**
1/2 oz. **Light Rum**

Shake equal parts of the tequila, vodka and rum with ice and strain into a shot glass.

BULLSEYE

1 oz. **Blanco Tequila**   2-3 dashes **Tabasco**®

Rim a shot glass with a lime wedge. Add the Tequila and Tabasco® to your liking. Slam it back.

PURPLE NURPLE

1/2 oz. **Tequila**   1/4 oz. **Sloe Gin**
1/4 oz. **Blue Curacao**

Hand swirl over ice then strain into a chilled shot glass.

Sloe gin is a sweet, red-colored liqueur, which is flavored with sloe berries. These berries are the fruit of the blackthorn plums.

PRAIRIE DOG

2 oz. **Tequila**   1/2 oz. **Tabasco**®
1/2 **Rose's**® **Lime Juice**

Rim shot glass with salt, pour in tequila, Tabasco® and Rose's® Lime Juice. Serve as a shot.

BAJA SHOOTER

When you visit the Baja peninsula,
you can find the most authentic way to do a tequila shot.
How much tequila you use depends upon your day!

1 medium **Lime**, cut in half
Tequila or **Mezcal**

Take a lime half and push a hole into it with your thumb (protect your eyes from possible lime juice squirting). Pour tequila or mezcal into the hole. Suck the tequila and lime juice all at once, in one large gulp.

TEQUILA TRIVIA

- ❖ The town of Tequila was founded in 1530 by a Spanish Conquistador, Capt. Cristobal de Onate.

- ❖ The definition of tequila is *"the rock that cuts."* The phrase probably came from the fact that the town is surrounded by obsidian (a sharp rock that was created by hot lava).

- ❖ The name **agave** comes from the Greek word for *"noble."*

- ❖ Sauza's Hornitos derives its name from the *horno,* the traditional stone or brick oven used to soften piñas.

- ❖ There are 136 species of agave in Mexico and about 30 different alcoholic beverages made from agave.

OTHER DRINKS WITH SPIRITS

MEXICAN MARTINIS

1 cup very **Dry Vermouth**
4 cups **Gin** or **Vodka**
12 **Ice Cubes**
Pickled Jalapeños

Place vermouth, gin or vodka and ice in a cocktail shaker. Shake well to chill. Strain into martini glasses. Place jalapeño on a toothpick and add to each glass. Makes 6 cocktails.

CANYON MIST

8 scoops **Vanilla Ice Cream**
3 tbsp. **Crème de Menthe**
2 tbsp. **Brandy**
3 tbsp. **Triple Sec**

Place all ingredients in blender and mix on lowest speed. Serve in mugs. Serves 4.

BLOODY MARIA'S

2 1/2 cups **Tomato Juice**
2 cans (12 oz. each) **V-8® Vegetable Juice**
3/4 cup **Lime Juice**
1 Tbsp. **Worcestershire Sauce**
1/2 tsp. **Tabasco® Pepper Sauce**
1 tsp. **Celery Salt**
Vodka

Combine and blend on low speed in blender. Chill well. When ready to serve, add 1 part vodka for every 2 parts mix. Serves 8-10.

MEXICAN EGGNOG

1 quart **Eggnog**
1 cup **Rum** or **Brandy**
Cinnamon Sticks

Combine the eggnog and rum, or brandy, and chill. Serve with cinnamon sticks. Serves 5.

NON-ALCOHOLIC DRINKS

SUN TEA

Sun tea is a great favorite in Mexico. Don't be discouraged from brewing delicious tea if you haven't seen the sun recently. Follow the same directions and allow the teas to brew for several hours in the refrigerator.

2 quarts **Cold Water**
1/2 cup loose **Tea** or 6 **Tea Bags**

Combine water and tea in a large jar. Cover and place in sun or in refrigerator for 6-8 hours. Strain tea. Add lemon or lime slices, if desired.

Mexican Hot Cocoa

1/4 cup **Cocoa**
1/4 cup **Sugar**
3/4 tsp. **Cinnamon**
1 quart **Whole Milk**
1/3 cup **Heavy Cream**
1 tsp. **Vanilla**

Combine cocoa, sugar and cinnamon. Set aside. Heat one cup of milk until bubbly; stir in cocoa mixture, mix with whisk until smooth. Gradually stir in remaining milk so slow boiling continues. Remove from heat, stir in cream and vanilla. Mix well. Makes 5 cups.

Not all of Mexico's favorite beverages contain spirits. Mexican coffee and chocolates are delicious and fresh fruit punches are widely available. Flavored teas are becoming popular everywhere and are wonderful served hot or cold.

MEXICAN CHOCOLATE II

4 cups **Milk**
4 oz. **Sweet Chocolate**
1/8 tsp. ground **Cinnamon**

Heat milk and chocolate together until chocolate is melted. Stir in cinnamon. Whip until frothy with hand mixer or in a blender. Serve warm. Serves 4.

COFFEE POT TEA

To make tea, use a regular coffee maker using two filters instead of one, as for coffee. For a 10-12 cup coffee pot, place 8 tablespoons of loose tea in the filter. Add a full pot of bottled water and brew.

Serve tea hot or cold—over crushed ice or ice cubes.

SPICED COFFEE

This is also delicious served over ice.

4 cups bottled **Water**
1/3 cup dark **Brown Sugar**
1/2 cup instant **Coffee**
4 **Cinnamon Sticks**

Combine water and sugar in medium saucepan. Bring to a boil and stir until sugar is dissolved. Reduce heat to simmer, stir in coffee and simmer 1-2 minutes. Pour into mugs, add cinnamon sticks. Serves 4.

MEXICAN RANCH COFFEE

10 cups **Cold Water**
5 tbsp. **Ground Coffee**
1 tsp. **Sugar**
Whipped Cream, if desired
Ground Cinnamon, or **Cinnamon Stick**, per mug,
   if desired

Combine first three ingredients and bring to a gentle boil.
Remove from heat and let ground settle for 5 minutes.
Pour through strainer into mugs, add whipped cream to
which ground cinnamon has been added, if desired.
Makes 10 cups.

SUMMER COFFEE

This is a great dessert coffee on a warm summer evening.

Follow the directions for **Mexican Ranch Coffee,** omitting the whipped cream. Place coffee in blender, add one pint **Vanilla** or **Coffee Ice Cream.** Liquefy in blender. Serve in mugs.

COCOA COFFEE

1 package **Hot Cocoa Mix,** any flavor
1 cup hot **Coffee**

Prepare hot cocoa mix according to package directions, substituting coffee for the hot water. Stir well to dissolve cocoa mix.

ReFResco de FResas

Strawberry Drink

1 basket **Strawberries**, hulled and sliced
6 cups **Water**
1/2 cup **Sugar**
Crushed Ice
Mint Sprigs (optional)

Combine strawberries with 2 cups water in blender and purée. Add remaining water and sugar and mix thoroughly. Cover and refrigerate. To serve, pour over crushed ice in tall glasses. If desired, garnish with mint sprigs. Serves 6.

Recipe:_____

From:_____

Ingredients:

_____   _____

_____   _____

_____   _____

_____   _____

_____   _____

Directions:_____

_____

_____

_____

_____

Recipe:_____

From:_____

Ingredients:

_____   _____

_____   _____

_____   _____

_____   _____

_____   _____

Directions:_____

_____

_____

_____

ABOUT THE AUTHOR

Sean Hoy's bartending career began in 1998 when Gordon Zuckerman, owner of Resorts Suites in Scottsdale, Arizona, stopped Sean after one of his brilliant comedy performances in a popular regional improvisational comedy troupe. Mr. Zuckerman declared Sean's dynamic personality would bring a fortune as a bartender. The following Monday Sean began his bartending career.

Sean's witty talents complemented his bartending skills at Resorts Suites for two years. Taking a break from the desert, he transplanted his refreshing bartending techniques to Chadron, Nebraska, managing the Ridgeview Country Club's bar. However, he was soon lured back to Arizona as lead bartender for the Scottsdale Plaza Resort. By 2006 Sean had found his home at The Saguaro Blossom, a scenic poolside dining experience, at The Four Seasons Resort Scottsdale at Troon North. In addition to Sean's outrageous and entertaining customer service that shines in his Saturday Salsa/Margarita Shows, his bartending leadership returned the coveted Hospitality Games Trophy to The Four Seasons.

When not bartending Sean puts his comic artistry to work in ink, as a professional cartoonist. This book's illustrations are evidence of his artistic skills and Sean has been published in many prominent magazines. *The Saturday Evening Post, Protooner, Illinois Medicine EXPRESS, American Legion Magazine,* and *The Arizona Republic* is a partial list of publications that have carried his political and satirical cartoons. Sean offers a hilarious collection of his work in *OFF COURSE Golf Cartoons,* with three more in progress including, *OUT of The CUBICLE Office Cartoons and Memos.*